Nirvana

GW00706157

Nirvana

Paul Haus

ORION

AN ORION PAPERBACK

This is a Carlton Book

First published in Great Britain in 1993 by Orion Books Ltd.
Orion House, 5 Upper St Martin's Lane, London WC2H 9EA

Text and design copyright © 1993 Carlton Books Limited
CD Guide format copyright © 1993 Carlton Books Limited

All rights reserved. No part of this publication may be reproduced, stored in a retrieval
system or transmitted, in any form or by any means, electronic, mechanical, photocopying,
recording or otherwise, without the prior permission of the copyright holder.

A CIP catalogue record for this book is available from the British Library.

ISBN 1 85797 570 7

Edited, designed and typeset by Haldane Mason
Printed in Italy

THE AUTHOR
Paul Haus
Respected author, Paul Haus, has worked as a professional music writer for the past fifteen years,
having been inspired to put pen to paper by the "do it yourself" mentality propagated by the punk
rock explosion of 1976. He met and interviewed many of the world's top rock bands and claims
he was inspired to write about Nirvana "because Kurt looks so fetching in a dress."

contents

Introduction

Nirvana's ascendancy to the peak of the music industry is one of the most surprising, yet electrifying, of modern times. From the ignominious roots of the backwaters of Washington, the musical vision shared by teenage friends Krist (the original European spelling of his Christian name, re-adopted last year) Novoselic and Kurt Cobain has blossomed into being at the forefront of a musical renaissance that comes from the heart and soul, ignoring trends, fads or commercial potential.

The band's second album (and major label début), NEVERMIND, has thrust its way into the consciousness of anyone who ever held rock music to be of any importance whatsoever. Its combination of instantly accessible melodies and fearsome guitar assault has resulted in worldwide sales in excess of 5 million, while the personal tensions within Nirvana have been put under the media microscope.

Now, with the much-anticipated and controversial release of the third album, IN UTERO, all eyes are watching to see whether the band can sustain their creative impetus and not crumble under the pressures of a world that has gone Nirvana crazy. Whatever the outcome, it's going to be a very interesting ride!

CHAPTER ONE

Here we are now, entertain us

Seattle is a four-letter word in all but spelling. What was once a by-line for the most exciting, creative, uncompromising and raw music to have emerged in the last decade has now become just another industry buzzword for a means of packaging rebellion and foisting it upon a record-buying public that's in it for the short haul. Sure, it may have been bizarre that a groundswell of musical prick-kicking could have sprung up in the sleepy north-western seaport and taken on the world, but at the end of five years of madness, it seems like the corporate whores have shifted ground in geographical terms, while the ethos remains the same. Take a scene from the underbelly that manages to rise to the surface against all the odds, add a sprinkle of that good old inoffensiveness dust and bingo! World-wide acceptance for all.

It's come to something when bands like the Screaming Trees are major label fodder, when the Spin Doctors are defined as grunge and when every high street store from London to Sydney has its grunge fashion accessories pushed to the fore in the display window. 'Smells Like Teen Spirit'? Smells like good ol' greenbacks to me.

It's easy to sink into a quagmire of remorse and cynicism about exactly what the Seattle music explosion of the late Eighties has really achieved. Has anything in fact changed? Has anything of lasting value

emerged that has wrestled musical expression any further away from blandola mainstream?

Well, for your answers, go back to 1986. The spirit of punk rock lived with the peroxide preening of Billy Idol and his sanitized attempts at rebellion. John Lydon once christened the Bromley boy "the Perry Como of punk" and with the likes of 'Rebel Yell' he wasn't far off the mark. Hard rock wasn't faring much better with the likes of LA's terminally terrible Ratt heading a plethora of third-rate Aerosmith copyists. If rock never died, it was at least in very great danger of suffering a coronary.

Seven years later you might look at the surface and claim that nothing much has really changed. Pearl Jam have provided an MTV face for the

Kurt Cobain—punk's last anti-hero.

Chris Novoselic, Nirvana's 6-foot 7-inch bass player.

shit! It's still the same old battle cry: "Here we are now, entertain us." For God's sake! But is it really that depressing, that much of a rejuvenation of the old rules perpetrated by the old school? Has the corporate stranglehold won out over everyone again?

I'm not altogether convinced that something good hasn't come out of this. After all, you have Nirvana.

Selling 9 million

The second album the band released, NEVERMIND, has sold over 9 million copies worldwide. It's a lot of records. It's up there with Guns N' Roses and their quintessentially LA vision of partying, Jack Daniels and silicone implants. It's stadium figures. Selling 9 million, with a huge slice of that tally being chalked up in your homeland, gains you a lot of power.

Nirvana have used the power of music and the power of a high-finance industry to fight from the inside. It's the only way you can do it. Some with per-

Seattle scene. Alice In Chains just labour away under the weight of knowing that they're nothing more than a hoary old heavy metal band. The only difference between the new school and the old school is that these days there are bands being signed to major labels who are shit and can't play. Back in the bad old days they were just

spectives far narrower than is good for them gave it to the band good and hard for signing to a major label. It would have been possible to get the horrific message of a song such as 'Polly' across by being signed to some two-bit indie outfit with every good intention and not a hope in hell of being heard—sure! There's still no guarantee that Nirvana's message is being heard. No guarantee that the fact that they ` have reclaimed the power and intensity of the rock guitar from those who bastardized its potential has been noted where

From the left: Dave Grohl, Kurt Cobain and Chris Novoselic.

it matters. But there is a chance. There's a belief in something more than the rock star ethos that Nirvana have clung to. Doggedly. With some price to pay. Yet it's 1993, and Nirvana are right in the eye of the storm. They haven't compromised.

It would have been easy for vocalist/guitarist Kurt Cobain, bassist Chris Novoselic and drummer Dave Grohl to have wilted under the pressure. No one would dare say it. No one would dare intimate that the pressure is on to reproduce. But once you've had major success the insidious and unspoken urge to achieve is underlying. It must weigh heavy on the collective heads of a trio who wilfully went against the grain of the American way. Such major achievement for a bunch of self-confessed slackers undermines a whole nation's accepted belief that getting on is the prime mover. Not "getting it on"—just doing it because it's what you feel you've got to do. Nirvana are as radical as pop music is going to get in America.

A genuine passion

The band have been working on IN UTERO, the third album proper, and they've been doing it the hard way. Recording it at Pachyderm Recording Studios in unfashionable Minnesota, Nirvana have taken the deliberately tough option of enlisting notoriously difficult producer Steve Albini to guide them through the minefield that they face. The band are aware of the pressure they're under. Working titles for the record have been I HATE MYSELF AND I WANT TO DIE and the sardonic VERSE CHORUS VERSE. It's not been easy.

NEWSWEEK magazine has run a full-page article detailing comments made by

Nirvana—self-confessed slackers who've succeeded against the odds.

**The grunge look,
© K. Cobain.**

> "We have 100 per cent control of our music. What makes a good record is the songs, and until we have the songs recorded the way we want them, Nirvana will not release this record."
>
> **Kurt Cobain**

Albini in an interview conducted for the CHICAGO TRIBUNE which claimed that Geffen had put pressure on the band to "clean up" tracks recorded by Nirvana with him. Nirvana reacted angrily, with Cobain issuing a statement: "We have 100 per cent control of our music," and that this was even written in their contract. He continued, saying that Steve Albini had made a career out of being anti-rock establishment, but being commercial or anti-commercial is not what makes a good rock record. "It's the songs, and until we have the songs recorded the way we want them, Nirvana will not release this record."

It restores a little bit of your faith in rock that, at this juncture, after all that has gone down in the Nirvana case history, there is some integrity in the band's motivation. They're talking about music with a genuine passion and a genuine feel for wanting to create something which challenges, which excites in the same way that NEVERMIND did, only differently.

It's hardly as if Nirvana have nothing else to talk about—they're as newsworthy as just about anything else on the planet right now. There's scandal—Cobain's marriage to Hole's enfant terrible, Courtney Love, for starters. The Sid and Nancy of grunge. There are the stories of Kurt's supposed hero-in addiction, the talk that Court-ney was still on the drug while carrying the couple's first child, Frances Bean. There are Kurt's well-documented comments regarding his feelings on homo/bisexuality.

There's enough to keep rags feeding off that tittle-tattle for months—and many have. But no matter how much bullshit Nirvana are trying to ride, there is a commitment to the fact that music can mean more than just a collection of dumb fist-punching anthems.

**Rocking at Reading
in 1991.**

Success wasn't in the game plan

Nirvana are confused. That's their appeal. They shun the glitz and the glamour of the accepted rock industry parameters, yet in Cobain they have the most recognizable icon of the generation. They abhor the self-indulgent excesses of your typical stadium band, yet they admit to having been strung-out more than is healthy. They scorn the "kick ass" mentality, yet they destroy their instruments on stage with an absurd glee. They buck against what MTV and its blandola, mind-numbing approach makes of people, yet their videos are among the highest-rotated clips on the network. If there's one thing that Nirvana have learned from this oddball merry-go-round, it's that subverting from the inside is not an easy task to undertake.

Hardest of all for the band is coming to terms with what they have achieved. It's all very well railing against the powers, the intangible, shadowy half-figures who control from behind closed doors, but what do you do when you suddenly find that some of that power is in your own hands? The biggest difference between Nirvana and a myriad other young soul rebels who have come before them is that you really believe that global success wasn't in the game plan. While the Pistols were as calculated as can be, Nirvana

band" wouldn't touch the hearts and imaginations of so many millions of people across the globe.

Very much for real

The logic behind why it was Nirvana is convoluted and complex. In the right place at the right time? That has something to do with it. Putting things into songs which hadn't been expressed as concisely or sincerely in a long, long time? Certainly. But perhaps the main reason why Nirvana's star has shot into the ascendant with such incandescent ferocity is that the record-buying public felt almost as one

Whoops! Nevermind...

just stumbled into the spotlight, blinking uncomfortably when they were caught in its full glow.

Dave Grohl, the least vocal and high-profile of the trio, sums up the band's approach to the mythological status which it now carries: "We are not the resurrection of Christ," he opines. "We're just another fuckin' band." Which is true, to a point—but "just another fuckin'

> **"We are not the resurrection of Christ. We're just another fuckin' band."**
> **Dave Grohl**

> **"If anything, our success gave me a dose of humility, the realization that we're just as normal and fucked-up as everyone else."**
> **Dave Grohl**

that this was a band that was very much for real. While there will always be fans who want their icons to be as far removed from their own existence as possible—the rock star as escapist attraction—there is now a huge mass of people who need and demand that their bands relate to where they're at. The Nineties are hard.

Gone is the excessive optimism and boom mentality of the early to mid Eighties. The Nineties are austere and, above all, confusing. Grohl again: "If anything, our success gave me a dose of humility, the realization that we're just as normal and as fucked-up as everyone else."

Nirvana never look as if they're giving us answers, they look like what they are— three young men from typical backgrounds, with typical problems and typically muddled perspectives. They just happen to have a larger ear waiting to hear them than most. And they have a lot more money!

It's been a rollercoaster ride for the band, and probably what's made it appear even more weird is the fact that they had been ploughing their own merry and unexceptional furrow for some considerable time before NEVERMIND exploded and a few minds were blown with it. Consider that, in August 1991, less than a month before

NEVERMIND was released, Nirvana were stuck way down on the bill at the Reading Festival as just another band that people thought were quite cool. Nothing more, nothing less.

A year later the band were back to headline, battle-hardened by 12 months that would have fried the most adroit of social manipulators, never mind three ordinary guys from Hicksville, USA, armed with nothing more than a few minutes of music and the belief that the American Dream had crumbled into mere particles of dust.

Just another cog

Nirvana hadn't even signed with a major recording label until the end of 1990. Up until that time the band had been just another cog in the wheel of Sub Pop Records, the alternative and now hugely credible Seattle-based label run by Bruce Pavitt and Jonathon Poneman as an attempt to

Dave, Chris and Kurt: three guys from nowhere who blew minds with NEVERMIND.

Cobain is the most recognizable icon of the generation—a hard act to play when you're just an ordinary guy shunning the spotlight.

redress the balance against a glut of major label music that they saw as sanitized and unchallenging. With an intuitive ear for music, the label was busy building up a roster of acts such as Green River, Tad, Mudhoney and Soundgarden who could still find it in themselves to create guitar-based rock that didn't play by the supposedly established rules of the game.

Nirvana were certainly seen as an integral part of the label's musical voice, but there were hardly any signs apparent that this act was going to be the big one. Even when the BLEACH album was released in June 1989, the aspirations for the record and the band didn't stretch past being signed by a major label and bringing a little bit of something more to the world's not-so-eager ears.

"It looks like it's gonna be pretty easy to find a big deal," said Cobain at the time. "We've just got to try to keep from being fucked." What the scruffy, blond-haired frontman was thinking of at the time would have amounted to nothing more than the usual youthful commitment to retaining artistic integrity that all new acts harp on about. Most groups, once sucked in by the corporate mangle, prove themselves to be malleable in the

21

Here we are now

Absolute Nirvana.

search for sales to assure a career in music. Most acts might pay lip-service to a desire for autonomy while eventually being swayed by the need to deliver the goods. Little did Cobain know that the one thing that would really screw the band up wouldn't be the demands of a record company hungry for a financial return, but rather the totally unexpected and not a little scary pressure of dealing with unanticipated success before the seeds of self-doubt had become crystallized in the music.

On the rollercoaster

Victims of a rollercoaster that ran off the rails and went way beyond their control, that's Nirvana. If the band had known just how much their private lives would be investigated, examined and dissected, if they had known that they would be subject to litigation and lawsuits from opportunists claiming that the band's name had been stolen from an obscure Sixties band, that Killing Joke would try to take them to court over the alleged filching of a bass line, that their every move would be subject to detailed scrutiny, it makes you wonder whether they

> **"It looks like it's gonna be pretty easy to find a big deal. We've just got to try to keep from being fucked."**
>
> **Kurt Cobain**

would have had the strength to see it all through. The benefit of hindsight is a wonderful thing. Or is it? Because from the point of view of those who want to see popular music make some kind of a statement, try to change things or at the very least heighten public awareness of situations, there is every need for Nirvana. The cost of their art on their own private lives has turned out to be heavy and Nirvana find themselves in a situation not of their own making, yet a situation that they have to deal with none the less.

I guess it's pretty confusing when you become the band that knocks U2 off national Irish radio station 2FM's "best record" table after 6 years. You don't get much bigger than that—not unless you dethrone Michael Jackson's DANGEROUS from poll position in the BILLBOARD Hot 100 album charts. It's a heady atmosphere up there and the air is rare. Within the space of a paltry three years Nirvana have climbed from the bottom of an inordinately large pile to perch precariously at the very top. Now

Flash! Saviour of the Universe!

Nirvana have kept
their integrity intact
through their
meteoric rise.

the question is whether the band are going to fall off. What's weird is that there aren't too many people who would be glad to see them fall. Their integrity has remained intact, even withstanding a cover of 'Smells Like Teen Spirit' by Weird Al Yankovitch. If you've got the balls to get over that little trauma, then a little bit of bad-mouthing from Guns N' Roses doesn't seem too bad.

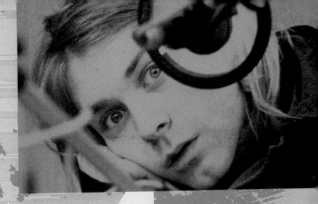

Kurt goes through his blue period.

Sixties influence

Nirvana have proved that they have enough about them to remain in the public eye for some considerable time to come. The vibes which they emanate draw comparisons with the Sixties. While the band's music leans more on the ferocity of punk rock and hardcore, Cobain could never deny the Beatles' influence on his melodic toplines.

However, it's in the band's willingness to confront authority and tackle real issues that the echoes of the politically-activated Sixties are most striking. For a bunch of under-achievers, Nirvana have probably heightened public awareness of contemporary issues more than anyone else on earth. Just witness Novoselic's interest in and desire to understand the Bosnian/Croatian conflict, even to the point where he's written an article for US magazine SPIN, outlining his thoughts on the problems in the former Yugoslavia.

All these elements merge into one to produce the most exciting band of our times, and certainly the most relevant. Yet with so much peripheral activity we

Kurt and Courtney wedded: blissed out!

should all be aware that it is one element above all others that has locked Nirvana's approach on to the hearts of the world like a laser beam. It's often forgotten, but it's the music. Without great music, the other issues become meaningless. Nirvana strike the right musical chord, marrying tunes with thunder.

"Here we are now, entertain us." Nirvana have provided us with more entertainment than anyone or anything else in today's youth culture.

The band's biggest secret weapon is that they connect—not just with a minority, but with the majority. That ability is worth its weight in gold and should never be underestimated. The band's most obvious soundbite turned the usual accepted notion of the group/audience relationship on its head: "Here we are now, entertain us."

Inadvertently or otherwise, Nirvana have provided us with more entertainment than anyone or anything else in today's youth culture. Hard as it may be to believe in the power of the individual in a corporate decade, Nirvana is the living proof that swimming against the tide isn't always a negative exercise. For it was from the humblest of origins that this unexpected success began.

Publicity and people focus on the peripherals—and forget Nirvana's core is its great music.

CHAPTER TWO

From despair to where?

If you come from Aberdeen, Washington, you're fucked—unless you're very strong-willed, very lucky, or both. It's a depressed little town, about 100 miles (160 km) south-west of Seattle, which survives mostly through the logging industry. It's a town in decline, it's seen better days and the future looks bleak. People don't like to talk about bleak futures. If that's all you've got to look forward to, best just to bury your head in the sand and get on with this painful thing called life.

It hadn't always been that way in Aberdeen. During the mid-nineteenth century, when the whaling trade was big, the

"No ideas are going through.
There's like a collective
unconsciousness there.
Just people in their houses,
rained out, drinking a lot.
A lot of drugs."
Chris Novoselic on Aberdeen

seaport was a thriving place, buzzing with sailors and the feel of opportunity. Wherever you get sailors coming into port you're bound to get whorehouses, and out of the ancient trade of prostitution there grew a small community. Chris Novoselic has been known to comment that Aberdeen's history has created a general feeling that the residents are a little ashamed of their roots in this isolated community and the overall air of depression has been assimilated into the very fabric of the town.

Unemployment is rife and the dissatisfaction of the residents seems curiously mirrored by the perpetually grey and rainy climate. The suicide rate in Aberdeen is more than twice the state average, already high in comparison to the rest of the

Portrait of the artist as a young hippy.

Opposite: An early incarnation of Nirvana. Left to right: Chad Channing, Kurt Cobain, Jason Everman and Chris Novoselic.

country. Aberdcen is not a creative centre in any way, shape or form. Greenwich Village and the bohemian art culture might as well not exist for anyone growing up there: "No ideas are going through," claims Novoselic. "There's like a collective unconscious there. Just people in their houses, rained out, drinking a lot. A lot of drugs." He describes the town as having no white collar workers, other than a few bankers and lawyers. The legal system consists of public defenders and prosecutors, with a few private lawyers doing divorce cases.

A hard town

This is the environment in which Novoselic and Kurt Cobain grew up in the Sixties and Seventies; a hard town, with no time for anyone with ideas or thoughts which transcended the deadbeat everyday. Cobain's mother was a secretary, his father a car mechanic—ordinary, everyday folk. Kurt's mother,

Wendy O'Connor, recounts that Kurt was a happy child with an above-average perspective of how the world was. He was very tuned in, full of joy at the prospect of every new day, every new experience to be had, without ever being fooled into thinking that the world itself was an entirely sunny place. In a way, it scared her, because he had perceptions like she had never seen in a small child before. He had life figured out very young, and knew it wasn't always fair. She describes him as being focused on the world—for example, he would be drawing in a colouring book while the news was on, but he was attuned to it, even when he was just three and a half. He knew all about the Vietnam war.

Within a happy home environment, young Kurt could have had a very fulfilling childhood. However, there were two elements which conspired to rob him of his bliss. The first was the fact that

Bleached-out Cobain. He had life figured out early, without ever expecting it to be fair.

mother, father, uncles and grandparents, young Kurt soon became what he later referred to as something of a "juvenile". His differing outlook on life, coupled with the family unrest, made Kurt even more dislocated in his home town. His mother thinks that if he had been anywhere else he would have been fine—there would have been enough of his kind for him not to stick out so much. "But this town is exactly like Peyton Place. Everybody is watching everyone and judging, and they have their little slots they like everyone to stay in— and he didn't." It was a classic case of a young child needing to find escape and, in the culturally swirling America of the early Seventies, where else was Kurt going to retreat to other than into music?

A musical awakening

Up to the age of nine, all that Kurt was exposed to in the realms of contemporary music was the Beatles. It was when his father joined a mail-order record club

his parents divorced when he was eight years old. Wendy O'Connor says that the traumatic event changed his life, making the young Kurt extremely inward-looking, almost reclusive and difficult to bring out of himself.

Unsettled by the divorce and soon being shunted between

> **"I definitely have a problem with the average macho man, because they've always been a threat to me."**
>
> **Kurt Cobain**

Black Sabbath (*opposite*), Led Zeppelin (*left*) and Kiss (*below*), metal superstars whose powerful music provided a musical awakening for the young Kurt.

that albums by the metal superstars of the day—Black Sabbath, Kiss and Led Zeppelin—started to arrive in the post. Although the power of the music appealed, there was something missing in the chest-beating bravado of the likes of Paul Stanley and Robert Plant. It struck too close to the darker side of home life in Aberdeen, where to dare to be different was likely to incur the wrath of the average guy. "I definitely have a problem with the average macho man," says Cobain today, "the strong-oxen working-class type, because they've always been a threat to me." He felt he had had to deal with them for most of his life—being taunted and beaten up by them in school, and simply having to be around them and be expected to be that kind of person when he grew up. He felt closer to the female side of the human being than to the male—or, at least, the American idea of what

a male is supposed to be. "Just watch a beer commercial and you'll see what I mean."

Musically, Cobain's real awakening began with the Sex Pistols. Not that he had heard the music, but the pictures that he saw in magazines were intriguing enough: "I was looking for something a lot heavier," he recalls. "Yet melodic at the same time. Something different from heavy metal, a different attitude."

Although music was hardly what you might call top of the list of priorities in Aberdeen, unless it was purely as a functional form, a Friday-night backdrop to get stoned to, there was still one band in town that Cobain caught up with. He idolized the Melvins, drove their tour van, helped hump their gear and watched so many of their rehearsals that he reckons it ran into the hundreds. It was Melvins band leader Buzz Osbourne who befriended the 16-year-old Cobain, taking him to his first rock show, namely Black

Flag. Melvins bassist Matt Lukin, later of Mudhoney, reckoned that the youngster was blown away.

The first band

The experience solidified in Cobain's mind the desire to make his own music, an ambition which came part way to being fulfilled when Osbourne introduced him to a gangling, awkward guitarist called Chris Novoselic. To make some money the two of them joined together with a bassist (who eventually had to quit after losing his fingers in a logging accident) and formed a Creedence Clearwater Revival covers band. The two pals' confidence grew and things began to come together in the autumn of 1986, when Cobain and Melvins drummer Dale Crover recorded a demo titled 'Fecal Matter'. Novoselic was added as the band's bassist, Cobain moved to guitar and Aaron Burkhart was enlisted as drummer. Names for the group came and went with alarming regularity, with the pick of the crop being Ed, Ted, Fred and Skid Row, before Nirvana was settled on and the band began gigging in earnest, drummers arriving and departing with a frequency only matched by Spinal Tap.

Opposite: **The early nucleus.**

Kurt—icon for a generation.

"I was looking for something a lot heavier, yet melodic at the same time. Something different from heavy metal, a different attitude."
Kurt Cobain

37

From despair to where?

Having finally been kicked out of whatever home he was staying in at the time because of his refusal to get a proper job, Cobain availed himself of any friend's couch that was free, and when nowhere was available, he slept under some of Aberdeen's less salubrious bridges.

It seemed like a hell of a sacrifice to make when the quality of the gigs being offered to Nirvana was less than impressive. The band played in run-down houses in the area to half a dozen stoners, none of whom liked the band. Undeterred, they began to venture further afield, gigging in nearby towns such as Tacoma and Olympia and aspiring to make the big time—a gig in Seattle!

Affirming his ever-increasing status as a definite outsider, a boy not at one with the staid and stultifying atmosphere of regular Aberdeen, Cobain took to customizing various properties in the town with bizarre graffiti. "Queer" was written on the side of macho four-wheel trucks and other favourite slogans designed to shock were "God Is Gay" and "Abort Christ". Eventually the police caught up with the itinerant youth, arresting him for spraying "Homosexual Sex Rules" on the side of a bank. The upshot was a $180 (£120) fine and a 30-day suspended sentence.

The Melvins, Cobain's inspiration.

Drunk and belligerent

Nirvana's major break came when the demo tape Cobain had recorded with Dale Crover was played to the boss of the Seattle independent label Sub Pop by one Jack Endino, the man who had produced the tape and who later went on to be a godfather of the burgeoning Seattle scene. Label boss Jonathan Poneman was intrigued by the ten tracks he heard and arranged to meet Cobain and Novoselic in a Seattle coffee house.

Cobain was excited to be associated with the label which boasted one of his favourite bands on the roster, namely Soundgarden. Novoselic, however, was surly and less than enthusiastic. "Drunk" and "belligerent" are two words used by Poneman to describe his behaviour. He signed the band anyway.

Soundgarden, a personal Cobain fave, also from the Sub Pop stable.

39

Left to right: Kurt
Cobain, Jason
Everman, Chad
Channing and Chris
Novoselic—the line-up
which didn't record
BLEACH, despite Jason
Everman being
credited as guitarist
on the album cover.

It took a year and two drummers for any recorded results of the agreement to see the light of day. 'Love Bug' (originally recorded by the Shocking Blues)/'Big Cheese', a limited edition single of 1000 for the label's singles club, was released in October of 1988 to less than ecstatic response. Poneman and his Sub Pop partner, Bruce Pavitt, started putting gigs the band's way in the Seattle area: "We played some kind of benefit show on a Sunday afternoon at the Central Tavern," says Novoselic. "We showed up, set up and nobody was there." So they left.

'Spank Thru' was released on the Sub Pop 200 3x12-inch box set compilation and began to elicit some interest, not least from BBC Radio's John Peel. 'Mexican Seafood' appeared on the C/Z Records 7-inch compilation TERYAKI ASTHMA VOL. 1 with Melvins drummer Dale Crover performing.

Bleach

Of course, the big moment that the band had been waiting for arrived in the shape of BLEACH, the début Sub Pop album, recorded in late 1988 and released in June of 1989. The album was recorded in the spirit which has never left Nirvana; cheaply and with attitude. With producer Jack Endino at the helm, the album was recorded with drummer Chad Channing (although Dale Crover played on two numbers, 'Floyd The Barber' and 'Paper Cut'). And the entire cost of the recordings? Just $606.17 (£404.11)! Guitarist Jason Everman, now of Mindfunk, was credited as a guitarist on the album, despite the fact that he didn't actually play on any tracks.

Bleach reaches Britain

BLEACH was released in the UK on the Tupelo label to generally enthusiastic applause. It's almost impossible to look back on reaction at the time with any kind of rationale, but let's get it into perspective. BLEACH was liked, but it was not seen as the second coming. It was seen as more bizarre for the fact that Cobain

Mmm, nice trousers!

was spelling his name as "Kurdt Kobain" and that there were some pretty kooky titles such as 'Mr. Moustache' and 'Scoff'. There was potential in them there grooves, but no-one was getting too excited. UK's NME could barely muster a half-page spread on the band, while at the other end of the musical spectrum that the band were about to career across, metal mag KERRANG! awarded BLEACH three out of five and claimed that Nirvana should be taken with "a pinch of napalm and a lot of toilet paper"!

Although there were some rumblings of things happening up in Seattle, there is no way that Nirvana were being heralded as the hippest kids on the block. Mudhoney, and Soundgarden to a lesser degree, were being touted as the ones to watch. Nirvana were interesting, but very much coming up on the rails rather than streaking past the winning post.

Cobain, frontman for a moderately successful group when BLEACH was released—but at the time, most eyes were on Mudhoney and Soundgarden.

CHAPTER THREE

Bleach bums

With Jason Everman
ensconced in the
band's touring line-
up, Nirvana had no brighter
ideas about what to do with
the piece of vinyl that they had
conjured up than to get out
there and promote it in the
time-honoured fashion. Touring
to excess and not a date more
was the way forward and the
band set out on their first cross-
America stint. Money was tight,
which is hardly what you'd call
shocking, and the band have
stories to tell of the usual
undernourishment and under-
privilege. That's a story a million
groups could bore you with.

By the time the tour came to
an end in New York, Everman
was gone and Nirvana were down

**Sonic Youth,
gurus of the indie
scene, Nirvana
touring mates and
seminal influence.**

to a three-piece for a European tour with labelmates Tad. Again, tour support was minimal. The band were raking in an almighty £70 ($105) per night across Europe and although the reviews were positive and gurus of the indie scene Sonic Youth were quick to sing their praises, there was plenty more trauma awaiting them. BLEACH was creating a stir in the murkiest waters of the hardcore independent scene, but the strange blend of intense guitar power with poppy toplines with which the band would eventually break open the floodgates was still in its embryonic stages. Easy listening it wasn't.

Still, 35,000 copies sold on an investment of less than a thousand bucks was making very sound business sense to Sub Pop, and the label began to initiate negotiations towards the end of 1989 to sign Nirvana to a seven-album deal. The carrot which was dangled before the band was a potential distribution deal with Sony Music (which

eventually failed to materialize) but, wary of such a long-term commitment to a label which was still, after all, only an independent, the band decided to take stock after five touring stints.

It seemed fairly obvious to Nirvana that there was sufficient interest in them to assume that a major label deal could be forth-coming, but as 1990 got into full

Tad, Sub Pop labelmates—would you share a tour bus with these men?

Dave Grohl became the band's new drummer in the autumn of 1990.

released in Australia on Waterfront Records' HARD TO BELIEVE double album, and eventually appeared in the UK after being licensed to Southern as a single set.

Dave Grohl arrives

By August the band were back out on the road in the US with STP and Sonic Youth, with hardy perennial Dale Crover providing temporary cover for the departed Chad Channing. The autumn saw a return to the UK and the arrival of drummer Dave Grohl to the ranks. Grohl was earning a crust with Washington D.C. hardcore outfit Scream, but when the band disintegrated, he flew up to Seattle to check out Nirvana on the advice of mutual friend Buzz Osbourne: "All I really had was a suitcase and my drums anyway, so I took them up to Seattle and hoped it would work. It did."

The UK tour was originally slotted in to promote the band's new 'Sliver' single, which had been recorded with drumming help from Mudhoney's Dan Peters, but various problems meant that the

swing there were drummer problems once again. A second visit to the UK, pencilled in for the spring, was cancelled and Channing departed the fold.

A cover version of the Kiss classic, 'Do You Love Me?', was

> **"All I really had was a suitcase and my drums anyway, so I took them up to Seattle and hoped it would work. It did."**
> **Dave Grohl**

record wasn't actually released until January of the following year. By this juncture, however, the band had six tracks which had been recorded earlier in the year with producer Butch Vig for a proposed Sub Pop album release. Nirvana decided that they could shop these demos around with a view to securing their own major deal, regardless of what the Sub Pop plans might

be. Of course, anyone who wanted to take Nirvana on would be forced to buy the band out of its Sub Pop deal, but the quality of the songs was so strong that the band had full confidence in their ability to get away.

If there was a question of selling out, then it was lost on Cobain. "I should feel real guilty about it," he said, continuing that he should be living out the old punk rock threat, denying everything commercial and sticking in his own little world, not really making an impact on anyone other than the people who are already aware of what he was complaining about. "It's preaching to the converted." Cobain's fine sense of irony was already being honed to perfection.

Signed to a major

The band's belief that the time was right to forge ahead with major label status and major label clout was confirmed when they flew to LA, secured the services of a lawyer and began to be courted by a

> "We feel that we're
> diverse and accessible
> enough to try to infiltrate
> into more than one
> market. We want to
> reach the Top 40."
>
> **Kurt Cobain**

whole host of majors. Geffen
eventually walked away with the
band's signatures, not least because
the band's touring mates and
staunch supporters, Sonic Youth,
were signed to the label and had
whipped up interest. Nirvana
received an advance of $287,000
(£190,000).

The group began to look at
potential producers for the second
album immediately. The obvious
delight which they felt at finally
having the financial capability to
really turn the band into exactly what
they wanted it to be coursed a new

wave of enthusiasm through them. The fact that a major label had seen fit to sign the band, and on their terms, proved to Cobain and Novoselic that their somewhat eclectic view of Nirvana music was beginning to become a vision which was shared by others.

Confidence was soaring: "We feel that we're diverse and accessible enough to try to infiltrate into more than just one market." They felt they could appeal to more than just the metal or the alternative rock markets and wanted to try to be mainstream too. "We want to reach the Top 40. Even if the whole of the next album can't get across to that type of audience there's at least a hit single or two in there."

Cobain was really starting to get a handle on what the potential for Nirvana could possibly be. Although the public were unaware of what had been happening in the band at this juncture, Cobain already had the songs which he recognized far outstripped anything the band had released previously.

More than an underground attraction

The main aim for the band was to allow themselves to break free of the clichéd, inverted snobbery of the underground scene that they had spent so long in. Nirvana's potential was to be so much more than just another underground attraction and Cobain was at ease with his art enough to express his broader

The new, seminal line-up—from left: Chris, Dave and Kurt.

Opposite: **Major deal mindblower.**

49

The Smithereens have made it—Kurt Cobain is a fan!

The metaphorical gloves were off and the Nirvana express train was beginning to gather momentum.

The new record

With Cobain's avowed love of REM to the fore, the band made the audacious move of trying to enlist the Athens band's producer, Scott Litt, to work on NEVERMIND alongside Southern pop producer Don Dixon. Nothing came of the proposed alliance and the job ended up with Butch Vig, a little-known producer who had spent the Eighties working with little-known acts such as Killdozer, Tar Babies, Die Kreuzen and Laughing Hyenas. None of the records had achieved even minuscule success, but one Kurt Cobain had been listening. Lucky break!

Nirvana headed out to the laid-back pleasure spot of Van Nuys in California to begin work at Sound City studio with Vig at the helm and Slayer man Andy Wallace ready to mix. Although the band had motored on a quantum leap from the days of BLEACH and its $600 (£400) bill,

musical canvas: "We're finally coming out of the drains and saying 'we like pop music'," he told the NME in January 1991. He went on to admit that he liked REM and the Smithereens and was not afraid to say so any more, so if Nirvana wanted to write a song in the style of REM or Godflesh they would do so.

> **"I think *BLEACH* is a great record, but there was a very fine line between going too commercial and keeping it too raw."**
> **Butch Vig**

"I think BLEACH is a great record, but there was a very fine line between going too commercial and keeping it too raw." For NEVERMIND, Vig wanted to maintain an intense live band sound that would capture the way that Nirvana were playing at the

REM, the megaband it's OK to like— Nirvana do.

the final cost of recording NEVERMIND was minimal by major record company standards—the total bill, including living expenses, mastering and Butch Vig's fee, was $135,000 (£90,000).

According to Vig, the recording process was fairly smooth, with nothing more than the usual tantrums that anyone experiences when creative people get in a room together. In retrospect, Vig felt that there was definitely something happening with the record, something that was going to make it much more than BLEACH had been: "I tried to make the record more focused than BLEACH," he explained.

time, "which I think I accomplished."

'Smells Like Teen Spirit'

From the earliest stages of the recording, Vig was constantly drawn to one song. Driving round Los Angeles with very rough mixes blaring out of the stereo, he would catch himself constantly rewinding to one particular track. A strummed, clean electric would suddenly be interrupted by a furious avalanche of noise and intensity, before the tune settled down into a curiously laid-back verse. This constant ebb and flow, this battle of dynamics, kept up throughout the song and fitted so perfectly, so seamlessly, that Vig knew it was a winner. This was 'Smells Like Teen Spirit'.

Vig knew that he wasn't alone in the good feeling that he harboured for the number. Everyone who heard the rough mix was blown away by it and, although the band were keener on 'Lithium', Vig was determined

that 'Spirit' would be the lead-off track on the album.

People were certainly excited about the record, but Geffen A&R man Gary Gersh, who had signed the band to the label, was trying to be realistic in his expectations for it. Nirvana had been signed on much the same premise as their elder musical brothers, Sonic Youth—good credibility for the label, any big sales very much a bonus.

The band were shipped over to Europe to play a few festival warm-ups, including the 1991 Reading Festival. Nirvana appeared midway through the Friday

Where's my contact lens?

***Opposite:* Smells like a hit record.**

Here she is—now, entertain her!

afternoon before Chapterhouse and were well-liked by the media fraternity who had managed to turn up that early in the proceedings.

Despite the confidence that the band felt for the new record, it still seemed as if most people were blissfully unaware of the explosion which was about to happen. Geffen originally pressed up a mere 50,000 copies of Nevermind for the initial release, on September 24, 1991.

Twelve real songs

It's amazing in retrospect to look back on the record and dissociate it from the circus that has grown around it, but most people who were introduced to the delights of Nevermind prior to release were aware that it was a strong album. From the plaintive, bitter tinge of 'Lithium', through the deceptively gentle 'Polly' (a harrowing tale of a defenceless rape victim) and on to the pure punk rock adrenalin rush of 'Stay Away', there was the irrefutable fact that this was a collection of 12 real songs. No matter what the style, from the dirtiest guitar attack to the most gentle acoustic strumming, Cobain had given full reign to his natural tendency to write melodies above everything else.

Reading Festival, 1991, just before the Nevermind explosion.

In retrospect, it's what put Nirvana two steps ahead of their underground competition. And yet there was nothing in the slightest bit vacuous about the record. NEVERMIND showed those with an outmoded punk mentality that you could write commercial songs with credibility, while proving to the hard rock fraternity that you didn't have to be a beer-swilling meathead to play music that was hard as nails and twice as spiky!

'Polly' was an important lyrical statement to make, and the band realized its validity: "It's a true story," said Chris. He relates the song as being about a young girl who was abducted by a man and driven around in his van. The man then tortured and raped her. The only chance she had of escaping was to pretend to come on to him and persuade him to untie her. "That's what she did, and she got away. Can you imagine how much strength that took?"

the new record proved that they had music to offer that was going to appeal to those very people—to a large degree the kind of people that Novoselic and Cobain had had to fight against back in Aberdeen. "Most of the new fans are people who don't know very much about underground music at all," said Cobain, shortly after the album's release. He described them as listening to Guns N' Roses and perhaps having heard of Anthrax. "I can't expect them to understand the message that we're trying to put across." But at least Nirvana had

Wind machines a go-go?

Nirvana's approach to the whole hard rock situation was intriguing. While they had little in common with hard rock bands in terms of presentation or attitude,

> **"Most of the new fans are people who don't know very much about underground music at all. I can't expect them to understand the message that we're trying to put across."**
> **Kurt Cobain**

Nirvana, a sensitive study.

got their attention on the music. The band hoped that, eventually, maybe their message would dig into their new fans' minds. Kurt didn't really expect it to, since it attacked the very people to whom Nirvana were selling their records. But "at the same time, it's not malicious, it's not meaning to put them down."

A video with impact

The fascination of Nirvana was beginning to build by the time the album was ready to be pushed out for public approval. It was the very contradictory nature of the band, it was the sense of confusion that they managed to translate into the songs so superbly, that was getting people fired up.

Nirvana's approach has always been confusing. There was no great game plan and yet everything for NEVERMIND was worked on hard. The band were notorious for being slackers in certain areas, but Cobain himself had the idea for the album sleeve, photographed the monkey on the back of the CD and felt sufficiently unhappy about the video for the first single, 'Smells Like Teen Spirit' to get into the editing suite and redo it himself. This was possibly a good move—the video for the lead track, perhaps more than anything else, was responsible for the album taking off in such a meteoric fashion. Director Sam Bayer opted to shoot the song in a mutated high school to reflect the punk-derivative lyric dealing with apathetic youth. There were slam-dancing students, tattooed cheerleaders and a thrash-hungry caretaker to contend with.

Possibly because it might have taken the MTV power-brokers

There is no such thing as tour madness!

back to their own rebellious punk youth, the video was immediately slated for heavy rotation. It was exactly the start that the band needed. In America MTV is omnipotent. It plugs bands directly into the hearts and souls of every kid in every town in the whole of America. If you can be seen by that amount of people and they like what you do, it's hard to see how you can fail. Nirvana stood out from the majority of the candyfloss rock that was receiving airplay and immediately struck a chord. It was really the biggest break that the band could have had and it put Nirvana in line for a shot at the big-time from day one.

Cobain knew the importance of MTV: "I expected our core audience to buy our record within the first couple of weeks and that sales would decline after that. But after I realized that we were on MTV, I suspected we would sell a lot more." Dave Grohl saw people looking at the video as if it was some monumental statement. "So many people think it's the epitome of this rebellious high school vibe."

Whatever the reaction to it, the video was the perfect introduction of the band to an audience utterly unfamiliar with Nirvana's history, politics, personnel

"I expected our core audience to buy our record within the first couple of weeks and that sales would decline after that. But after I realized that we were on MTV, I suspected we would sell a lot more."
Kurt Cobain

"Look ma. I'm on top of the world!"

even. It was becoming more and more appropriate by the day that the band's album sleeve would feature a baby underwater chasing a dollar bill tied to a hook—Nirvana, fledgling participants in the big rock game, would soon be lured by the almighty power of the dollar. It would be interesting to see whether first the public, and second the band, would be prepared to take the bait.

The back of the CD insert was to feature Cobain, Grohl and Novoselic, blurred and out of focus, with Cobain raising the middle finger in the typical American gesture of defiance. It's the kind of thing that any of a million US rock bands do week after week in press shots, but there's something about the anger in Cobain's face that suggests that this is something that's for real, rather than just an empty fashion statement. This was an indication of intent.

More blurred visions of Nirvana tour frenzy!

> **"I didn't think NEVERMIND would be that much different to BLEACH—just a progression."**
> **Dave Grohl**

Even on the eve of release, even with people being very positive about the songs, Nirvana were still unaware of the forthcoming furore. Dave Grohl just thought it would be like another successful independent record vibe. "I didn't think that NEVERMIND would be that much different to BLEACH— just a progression."

It was time for the band to find out exactly what lay around the corner for them. If the record worked, great. And if it didn't—well, you could always just say NEVERMIND!

Insanity assassins

> "That's what music is, entertainment. The more you put yourself into it, the more of you comes out in it."
>
> **Kurt Cobain**

The minute that NEVERMIND hit the streets, all hell broke loose. It was the most bizarre success story in modern musical history. Without any kind of promotional hype, without any big spend on the part of Geffen, the album suddenly began to rocket skywards. It entered the BILLBOARD charts at 144, climbed to 109 in its second week, shunted up to 65 then 35 and after only seven weeks in the charts had careered to the dizzy heights of Number 4. Within just six weeks the album had sold a million copies and all those who were involved were reeling with the shock of it all. Sure, everyone had thought that the

record was great, but there are loads of great records that appear and don't do anything. Cobain immediately tried to play down the significance of NEVERMIND's rise to the top by saying that the band were merely entertainers: "That's what music is, entertainment. The more you put yourself into it, the more of you comes out in it. You can't help but hear a little of your own personality screaming out sometimes."

Under the microscope

Looking back on such a statement, it appears clear that the alarm bells were already beginning to ring in Cobain's head as he foresaw the enforced responsibility, the microscopic attention that was going to be paid to his life. Nirvana were going to become public property, not just musically, but personally too— and Cobain didn't seem too happy about the prospect.

By November 1991, the band had hoiked up their gear and begun a six-month world tour. The astonishing speed with which NEVERMIND had been picked up by the public had meant that in less than two months since the release of the album the demands on the band

were unreal. In the UK 'Smells Like Teen Spirit' was released to coincide with the tour and scaled the dizzy heights of the singles charts, reaching a wobbler-inducing Number 7. The band

All hell broke loose with the release of NEVERMIND. Within seven weeks it was Number 4 in the BILLBOARD charts.

performed on UK TV's Top of THE POPS, affirming that here was a band with real pop potential.

Revelling in outrage

Novoselic was revelling in the outrage being caused by this underground band with a sudden overground haul of album sales: "We're a very, very heavy pop band," he said. "Like, if Cheap Trick were to have a lot of distortion in their guitars. That's about the closest you can get to it—if anything, we still consider ourselves a punk rock band." It seems as if the band were as confused by what was happening to them as anybody!

Still, the performances on the tour were electric and Nirvana's new-found status as the hottest property in rock was exploited to the full by an eager Geffen. TV appearances in the UK on JONATHAN ROSS and THE WORD astounded everyone with their brutality and urgency. Cobain in particular shocked (or thrilled) the viewers of the latter show by announcing that Courtney Love was "the best fuck in the world"!

Courtney Love, frontperson of Hole, another of the underground bands that was spawned in the same scene whence Nirvana had come, had already forged herself something of a minor reputation on the scene with outrageous behaviour that could

Courtney Love (*right*), "wild child" and frontperson of Hole (*opposite*).

> "We're a very, very heavy pop band. If anything, we still consider ourselves a punk rock band."
>
> **Chris Novoselic**

range from being a stripper to a heroin addict, depending on whose distorted views you might care to believe on any particular day.

Of course, once it had been revealed so publicly that the leader of the world's biggest new band was dating a so-called "wild child" it was all too much for the tabloid papers to take. Stories of such ludicrously exploitative proportions as not to

> **"I thought the album would sell 300,000 or 400,000 copies in 5 or 6 months. We really had no idea."**
> **Ray Farrell, Geffen**

Cobain joins the lemmingheads.

be worth delving into began to paint the relationship as a Nineties reincarnation of Sid Vicious and Nancy Spungeon's ill-fated liaison which resulted in both their deaths. Of course, it's nothing of the sort. For a start, Cobain is erudite, educated and to all intents and purposes a feminist. Cobain and Love met on the LA club scene and fell in love. What they did in their private lives, as individuals or as a couple, is irrelevant.

As the Nirvana success story began to unfold, every chance to create some scandal was grabbed by the media—especially

where the messy businesses of love and drugs were involved. As Cobain was to remark much later, everyone seemed to think that they couldn't possibly love each other since they were thought of as cartoon characters, because they were in the public domain. But this was something they were going to have to get used to.

Public property

Public property was exactly what Nirvana had become. By January 1992 they had achieved the impossible by managing to topple Michael Jackson from the top of the BILLBOARD album charts. In the last week of December alone, NEVERMIND sold 373,520 copies and still nobody had got a handle on why. The manager of the band, Danny Goldberg, suggested that the American public hadn't been satisfied with corporate, conventional rock stuff over the last couple of years. They had a yearning for something that felt new, not constantly trying to

Pearl Jam's Eddie Vedder—criticized by Cobain for being too commercial.

reinvent Led Zeppelin and the Rolling Stones. "I thought the album would sell 300,000 or 400,000 copies in five or six months," said Geffen's Ray Farrell. "We really had no idea."

Everywhere you turned to try to pin down why it was Nirvana, you kept getting the same response or, at the very best, half theories. All that you could really put it down to was the "right place, right time, right record". According to Cobain there never was an agreement between them and their label to go for massive promotion—it just happened. It was just organic, although it happened really fast.

The pressure mounts

Fast is not the word to describe what had happened to the band. And of course, as you might expect, there was a price to pay. By December of 1991 the pressure was starting to get to Nirvana, and to Cobain in particular. A European tour on which the band had set out with real intent disintegrated as Cobain's voice packed up just after the Transmusicales Festival in Rennes, France. It was just the old pressure of success business, and the success was getting to be ridiculous. Nevertheless, Cobain's voice problems can't have been too serious, as the end of the most insane four months in the band's life ended with a New Year's Eve performance at the 15,000-capacity Cow Palace in San Francisco, sandwiched in between Pearl Jam (whom Cobain had criticized for commercializing "alternative" music) and the Red Hot Chili Peppers. Nirvana stole the show, which summed up the year rather appropriately.

The following year commenced the way that 1991 had ended, with Nirvana mania still at fever pitch. An indication of just how far the band had come since the album was released was proved by the fact that they appeared on the highly prestigious SATURDAY NIGHT LIVE show in the US. Mainstream was the main vibe with Nirvana and there wasn't a damn thing that they could do about it. Novoselic was pretty much resigned to taking flak for a situation over which he had very little control. He said: "People always ask in interviews about the big sell-out question. And I'm like, well, just

Pressure? What pressure?

> **"Just because you make some money doesn't mean you're selling out."**
> **Chris Novoselic**

because you make some money doesn't mean you're selling out." In his view, starting to vote Republican on the grounds that they would take care of him as a rich person would be a sell-out.

Back on the road

The members of Nirvana were finally able to afford to reap some of the tangible rewards from their five years of graft. Time to sit back and enjoy the benefits. Well, almost.

Getting the most out of a guitar...

The end of January and February saw the band heading out on the road again, spreading their wings wider to embrace a whole world which decided it wanted to know Nirvana just that bit better. Australia and Japan were both treated to a taste of the live Nirvana spirit, and the sold-out 3000-capacity show in Sydney was indicative of the whole string of dates. Forty-five-minute bursts of extreme intensity were gratefully received by a throng who would probably have accepted anything from their heroes. It was a situation that worried Cobain, who knew that many of the crowd would be present for all the wrong reasons. Though he didn't want to go back and play clubs, he did feel he would like to get rid of the homophobes, sexists and racists in their audience. He knew they were out there and it really bothered him.

After the Japanese dates, in secret and without even Grohl or Novoselic present,

...involves a lot of activity...

Cobain and Courtney Love were married by a non-denominational female priest in Hawaii with only a roadie as witness: "It's like Evian water and battery acid," said Cobain of the relationship. And when you mix the two? "You get love. I'm just happier

...and emotional exhaustion. It's all too much!

than I've ever been. I finally found someone that I'm totally compatible with. It doesn't matter whether she's a male, female or hermaphrodite or a donkey. We're compatible."

Extra tracks

While Cobain poured a lot of his energies into his relationship with Courtney, it seemed as if the rest of the world was simply waiting for the next piece of tittle-tattle that would keep the name of the band in the news. It emerged that there were copies of NEVERMIND which had an extra track, 'Endless Nameless', included about 10 minutes after the finish of the album proper. In some ways it brought home the band's earlier naïveté, when the eyes of the world weren't so intently focused on them and when they could simply mess with things just for the hell of it.

Of course, any extra music from the band

was greeted as very big news indeed. Reissues and bootlegs had become very much the order of the day, with BLEACH being reissued in America on coloured vinyl. The band's control over their music was slipping away from them.

Bootlegs were proving to be a problem, according to Dave Grohl. While the band didn't mind live bootlegs, they did mind people picking up cassettes of four-track tapes of Cobain messing around with his guitar in his room. "The quality is shit and you find these things selling for a fortune in the record shops," Grohl complained.

Of course, where there's money to be made you will find people wanting a piece of it. There were even some reports of gangs of merchandizing bootleggers operating in the UK who were armed and certainly dangerous.

Domestic bliss

The official release of 'Come As You Are' on March 2 reached Number 10 in the UK

> **"It's like Evian water and battery acid. I'm just happier than I've ever been. I finally found someone that I'm totally compatible with. It doesn't matter whether she's a male, female or hermaphrodite or a donkey. We're compatible."**
>
> **Kurt Cobain**

singles charts to prove that the support for the band had hardly waned since their departure from UK shores. Meanwhile, back in America, the Cobains moved into an apartment in Los Angeles' Fairfax district and got down to the serious business of trying to create some domestic bliss. However, as the couple were going to learn very quickly, even when they tried to hide away from the all-seeing eyes of the press, there was no way that it was going to be possible to keep their names out of the headlines. The kind of success that the band had achieved always comes accompanied by minor and major irritants. Like the obviously unwell fan who insisted on phoning a number of magazines and reporting that Kurt was dead, while sending out mock press releases outlining the demise of the band. Like the censorship board in Washington state that suddenly decided in April that NEVERMIND should be banned on the grounds that it was erotic. (Chris Novoselic was so incensed by the verdict that he went on a protest march!) Like the incessant rumours that began circulating in the American press that both Kurt and Courtney were strung out, messed up and wired on heroin.

That was one rumour which the Cobains felt the need to quash. In an interview with Michael Azerrad at the LA apartment, Cobain tried to pass off his ill-health and gaunt looks

as due to a "stomach complaint". Having eaten next to nothing for two weeks, he was described as "strikingly gaunt and frail", cutting a figure far removed from the cheeky and slightly overweight chap who had posed for the NEVERMIND album photos. Stress due to overwork was produced as the reason for the illness and Cobain brushed off the talk of more deep-seated problems. "I'm going to get healthy and start over," he stated.

A profile in San Francisco's BAM magazine claimed that Cobain was nodding off in mid-sentence, and that his "pinned pupils, sunken cheeks and scabbed, sallow skin" pointed to something more serious than simple fatigue. However, Cobain protested that he didn't even drink any more because it destroyed his stomach, saying that his body wouldn't allow him to take drugs if he wanted to because he was so weak all the time. In his most direct

Left and opposite: As 1992 progressed, Cobain looked more and more ill.

"All drugs are a waste of time. They destroy your memory and your self-respect and everything that goes along with your self-esteem...I've found they're a waste of time."

Kurt Cobain

chance jumping on the ailing frame of the band to grab for some easy pickings. A British psychedelic band also named Nirvana, who signed to Island in 1967 and scored a solitary Top 40 hit the following year titled 'Rainbow Chase', tried to put a legal claim in motion for compensation for the unlawful use of their name.

It was also revealed that a Los Angeles band called Nevermind were financially recompensed when Nirvana's album was first released. In addition, individuals claiming to have written 'Smells Like Teen Spirit' and 'Come As You Are' approached the press in the States threatening legal action. The band put a brave face on in the wake of the allegations and a spokesman pointed out that some people will do anything for a fast buck. All kinds of cranks were coming out of the woodwork since the success of NEVERMIND, but the band were prepared to stand up in court against

1992 was a year of troubles, with vultures flocking for easy pickings.

statement yet on the subject, he announced: "All drugs are a waste of time. They destroy your memory and your self-respect and everything that goes along with your self-esteem...I've found they're a waste of time."

Troubles upon troubles

As if fate sensed that the band were at a particularly low ebb, troubles mounted upon troubles, with those with an eye for the main

anybody at all who chose to challenge them.

At the end of April, with rumours still rife regarding the private lives of the biggest celebrity couple in rock, the announcement was made that the Cobains were expecting their first child. The infant was due to arrive on August 8 and the couple were reportedly delighted at the prospect of parenthood.

Courtney's pregnancy meant the withdrawal of her band, Hole, from the summer's Reading Festival, but reports that Nirvana, due to headline one of the three days, would also withdraw were dismissed as rubbish. It was also announced that Hole had signed to DGC alongside Nirvana as it was the label "who best understood their need for artistic control and political freedom".

By the time that June came around, a short tour of Europe had been slotted in and the scale of the band's success was beginning to be questioned by the group's leader, while his wife's pregnancy became ever more advanced. At least Cobain could still react with genuine enthusiasm to the prospect of working with Grohl and Novoselic. He knew that he had a reputation for being a difficult, moody person, and

Chris dwarfs his guitar on stage.

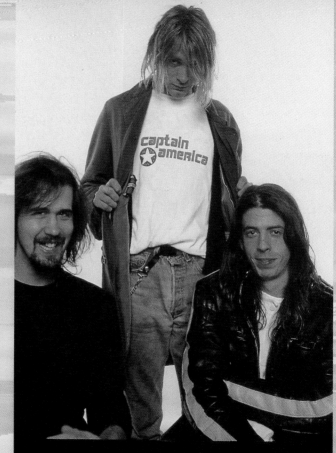

Kurt knew he had a reputation for being "this pissy, moody person", but he was genuinely enthusiastic about working with Novoselic and Grohl.

this made him feel that everyone was expecting him to freak out and develop some kind of ego or quit the band. But there was no way he was going to do that. He still liked playing with Chris and Dave and he knew that Nirvana's new songs were really good. It seemed that whatever problems the frontman might have had, he had managed to overcome them and was looking forward to the progression of the band.

Nirvana mooched back over to Europe to play dates in Ireland which were rescheduled from when Cobain's voice let him down at the end of 1991. Courtney accompanied her husband and hung around the venues looking very bored and very pregnant. It had also been decided that on their return to the States it would be time to up sticks and move back to the band's spiritual home of Seattle.

A change of style

It felt like there was change afoot. It was almost as if the

final throes of the madness that surrounded NEVERMIND were being acted out before the band moved on to the next phase in their career. Ideas, sketchy but interesting, had been mooted for the recording of the third album. Cobain was talking of recording at least half of it on an eight-track studio and

While Nirvana played dates in Ireland, Courtney hung around the venues, very bored and very pregnant.

taking some of the polish away from the band's sound. He had also cut his hair into a boyish, even geeky, style, and had adopted a very nerdy pair of specs. It seemed like he was looking for ways to distance himself from the long-haired, pissed-off punk who had risen to such world notoriety. The weight of responsibility was perhaps getting a little too much. What do you do when you become a role model for people who you never wanted to have an influence over in the first place? You get scared, that's what: "It really pisses me off," he claimed. "Because I'm kind of an example for people, and there are 9-year-old kids who are into our band, and if they think I take drugs and I think it's cool, then they are going to do it too."

Novoselic hit the dichotomy square on the head. The three all have ideas and opinions, which are just as available for people to consider as anyone else's. "But I don't

"I'm kind of an example for people, and there are 9-year-old kids who are into our band, and if they think I take drugs and I think it's cool, then they are going to do it too."
Kurt Cobain

think any of us feel qualified to be a spokesman for a generation." It was the old Nirvana self-defence tactics, employing self-deprecation in order to deflect any personal responsibility—just a perfectly understandable reaction when you have to live in the eye of the hurricane.

Cobain, too, was employing the self-same tactic to good effect when it came to the new album that was being mentally prepared. Apparently the songs to be recorded dated back to the NEVERMIND sessions: "They could be considered B-sides," he said. "So I guess the next album isn't going to be as good as everyone's expecting. I'm just too lazy to write new songs, so I guess people are going to have to put up with year-old B-sides."

Yet the overriding tone was one of optimism in the Nirvana

Onwards and upwards.

camp. Maybe it was due to the imminent arrival of the Cobains' baby. Maybe it was the fact that the band were good and rested for the first time in what had begun to seem like an eternity. Maybe it was just that they had stopped worrying about stuff that they couldn't control. Cobain was even optimistic about the future, explaining how his band's success had already opened the doors to a new generation of young go-getters. After all the triumph and the ensuing trauma it seemed that maybe, just maybe, things were gonna turn out fine after all!

Trouble returns

Yet as if to ruin the general feeling of content that was prevailing, Cobain was suddenly rushed to hospital in an ambulance. The reason given was that he was suffering from a weeping ulcer, a condition from which a spokesman close to him claimed he had been suffering for the last three years. Naturally, rumours immediately started flying concerning the supposed heroin problem, to

which a tart reply of "It's all bullshit. It's just because they're the most copy-worthy band in the world right now." was given. Still more problems reared their heads when the couple found their house flooded, with tapes of new songs destroyed in the mess. Courtney was also admitted to hospital as a result of problems with her womb.

'Lithium', the third track to be lifted from NEVERMIND in the UK, was released on July 13 to keep up the momentum, although it was patently obvious that the band had lost interest in the record.

There was talk of attempting to get the next record out for November, just so that the band could play some new material and work up a bit more enthusiasm for performance. Because of the bootlegging the trio had refused to play any new material at all, yet it was almost painfully obvious that their natural creative impetus was drawn towards dismissing the troubles of the past and getting on with the future.

Just when things seemed to be getting better, Cobain was rushed to hospital with a weeping ulcer.

CHAPTER FIVE

Excess success

August promised to be a big month. The Cobains' baby was due and there was a headline appearance at Reading to contend with. It was hard to believe, scary even, that only a year ago Nirvana had been nothing more than another groovy little act on a bill full of groovy little acts. Now the eyes of the world were firmly fixed on the Nirvana phenomenon—especially those of people wanting a piece of the band's considerable action.

Early in the month, the news broke that seminal Eighties rock band Killing Joke were suing the band. Bassist Paul Raven said that papers had been filed in Los Angeles claiming that the guitar riff from 'Come As You Are' was a direct copy of Killing Joke's 1985 hit, 'Eighties'. He expounded: "Basically, we have to prove that they've heard of us—the legal guys call it coercion. They have heard of us 'cos we've got Christmas cards from when they were a baby band. They've also namechecked us as an influence in loads of their early interviews."

The Killing Joke legal action, however, became nothing more than a minor irritant after the publishing of an interview in VANITY FAIR magazine which revealed that Kurt and Courtney had indulged in a drug binge while the latter was pregnant. A photograph was also printed of a heavily pregnant Courtney smoking a cigarette. In a fit of

Killing Joke—but
suing's not funny.

pique, Cobain pulled the band
out of a potentially triumphant
sold-out home town gig at the
15,000-capacity Coliseum, once
again showing just how fragile the
whole Nirvana situation could be.
Immediately rumours began to
circulate that the band would indeed
be pulling out of the Reading Festival
as well. The air was thick with
rumour and counter-rumour.

The arrival of Frances Bean
Frances Bean Cobain was born
on August 18, 1992. Both mother
and child were fine on arrival and the
more selfish of Britain's disaffected
youth breathed a huge sigh of relief
as the only cloud hanging over the
band's Reading Festival headline
appearance was removed. Still,
according to a cover story article
which ran in the NME to coincide

with the festival weekend, Kurt and Courtney's bliss might have been fine for them, but was turning into a right royal pain for everybody else. Dubbed "the Wicked Witch of the West" by one anonymous crew member, ignored by bassist Chris and wife Shelli, Courtney seemed more than aware of the hold she had on Cobain and was revelling in her position of power. Soundchecks, interviews, photosessions and so on were all put on hold while Kurt and Courtney were holed up back at the hotel. This kind of petulant rock star behaviour was supposed to be exactly what Nirvana had come to rid the world of. Meanwhile, Dave Grohl was trying very hard to be rational, saying that he didn't like to have people doing stuff for him. "I don't like to have runners go out and get me meals, I don't like to call down to room service and ask them to bring me up some cigarettes—it's just not normal."

The pressure shows

The pressure, according to Cobain, was beginning to tell on the shows. He admitted quite frankly to not enjoying

"I don't like to have people do stuff for me. I don't like to have runners go out and get me meals, I don't like to call down to room service and ask them to bring me up some cigarettes—it's just not normal."
Dave Grohl

The Cobains: Kurt, Courtney and new arrival Frances Bean.

Kurt Cobain in a
blond fright wig on
stage at 1992's
Reading Festival.

them as much as the previous year, that the heroin rumours were getting him down, and that he thought the four months the band had had off earlier in the year wasn't long enough for his liking!

And so to Reading, the show that everyone had been pinning their hopes on. And so to Kurt being pushed on stage in a wheelchair wearing a blond fright wig and a smock in mockery of his supposed state of health and probably his own wife. And so to millions of punters stretching as far as the eye could see getting well into it. And so to the band seemingly enjoying themselves for a change. And so to Nirvana annnouncing that this definitely wouldn't be the end of the band. And so, finally, to the end of all the NEVERMIND hoopla. The lights went down, and we all went home, with Nirvana having made everyone just that little bit happier than they were last year.

Back in the States, there was still no getting away from the spotlight, as the band scooped two categories at the MTV Music Video Awards, with Chris managing to give himself mild concussion at the show in Spinal Tap style by throwing his bass in the air and getting walloped on the head. As Nirvana were only too aware, it is indeed a fine line between clever and stupid!

Drug rumours

The re-release of BLEACH in the UK at the beginning of September gave Nirvana's newer fans the chance to check out what they had been missing. Of more concern to the band and their manager, Danny Goldberg, was a story which broke in the SUN on August 27 which claimed that Frances Bean had been born a drug addict. Apparently, the British daily newspaper had spoken to insiders at the Los Angeles Cedars Sinai Hospital who had claimed that the baby had been born "high on methadone" and that they had had to let her go cold turkey. Danny Goldberg, understandably, was

furious, saying that the paper had stepped over the line between sleazy and libellous and that he would probably sue: "I don't like to sue people for the fun of it," he retorted. "But I've personally seen the baby three or four times in the last week, and she's completely normal. All this stuff about cramps and chills is a complete and absolute lie."

"I don't like to sue people for the fun of it, but I've seen the baby three or four times in the last week, and she's perfectly normal. All this stuff about cramps and chills is a complete and absolute lie."
Danny Goldberg

Kurt and Courtney also issued a statement which read: "Because we were stupid enough to do drugs at one brief time, we realize that we opened ourselves up to gossip by people in the rock world who want desperately to pretend that they have some inside information on famous people. We never dreamed that gossip would be reported as if it were true without us even having the ability to comment on it, especially when the gossip reflects on such a personal and

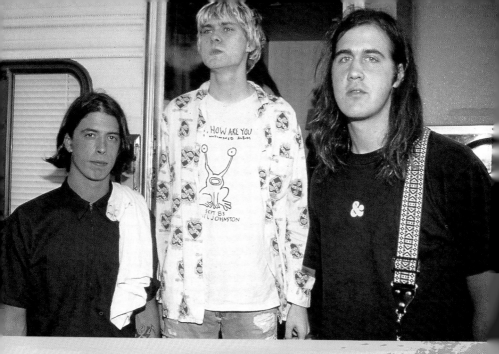

**Under the media
microscope.**

important event as the birth of our
first child."

In a further bid to diffuse the
increasingly irritating drug talk,
Cobain admitted to the LA TIMES

that he had used heroin while
condemning his own actions at
the same time. He admitted that
he chose to do drugs, but said he
had nothing good to say about

them, that they were a total waste of time. He was conscious that Nirvana had a lot of young fans and he didn't want to have anything to do with inciting drug use. "People who use drugs are fucked." He went on to reveal that he dabbled with heroin once or twice a year for several years and had developed "a little habit" earlier in the year. A doctor had prescribed methadone tablets when his stomach became upset after a detox programme and Cobain had been forced to return to the clinic for further treatment, which lasted somewhere in the region of a month.

Cobain claimed that the birth of his child had totally altered his perspective: "I can't tell you how much my attitude has changed since we've got Frances," he claimed, describing holding his baby as the best drug in the world. "I don't want my daughter growing up with people telling her that her parents were junkies."

More releases

Such intense rumour-mongering and scandal detracted wholeheartedly from the news delivered in October

> **"I can't tell you how much my attitude has changed since we've got Frances. I don't want my daughter growing up with people telling her that her parents were junkies."**
>
> **Kurt Cobain**

that there was to be a release of a home video of the band's 1991 European Tour with Sonic Youth. Titled 1991: The Year That Punk Rock Broke and directed by Dave Markey, the video showed nothing about the band of any interest or relevance and further went to show that anything with the Nirvana moniker attached to it, no matter how tenuously, was fair game for exploitation.

To combat such sensationalist behaviour, at least in the recorded field, details were released of a compilation album, to be called Incesticide, which would be released in the UK in December. It was to be a collection of early, obscure A and B sides, plus tracks culled from UK's Mark Goodier and John Peel Radio One sessions and three unreleased numbers from 1988 and 1989. In addition, there was talk of a shared single with Jesus Lizard, an idea that had been mooted long before Nirvana burnt off into the stratosphere.

Just for good measure, rumours flew thick and fast that Cobain was to produce the Melvins' first album for Atlantic, as a repayment for the

"I have never spoken
to Nirvana. I have
never spoken to their
management company.
I have never spoken to
their record company.
They have never
contacted me in
any way."
Steve Albini

Live wired!

inspiration they gave him back in the mid-Eighties. And even more interestingly, producer Steve Albini was so incensed at talk of his producing the next Nirvana record that he issued a statement which read: "I have never spoken to Nirvana. I have never spoken to their management company. I have never spoken to their record company. They have never contacted me in any way."

'In Bloom' was released as a single on November 30, while INCESTICIDE finally appeared on December 14 to reviews that basically hit the nail on the head. Some good, some bad, some baffling. But what do you want from a collection of odds and sods designed to keep the bootleggers at bay? And so 1992 blended seamlessly into 1993, and Steve Albini suddenly emerged as the man who, after all, had been chosen to produce the record.

The year of 1993 started pretty much the same as the year of 1992 in the musical world. Kurt and Courtney were talking to the papers, caught in the Catch 22 situation of talking to set the record straight and then finding that it just made things more crooked.

Courtney was still upset about being featured in VANITY FAIR, heavily pregnant and smoking a cigarette: "Fuck you, everybody smokes during their pregnancy," she ranted. Not true, although you get the gist, but surely, after a year of this constant media attention, the young woman would have known better than to let them do that to her. Not the brightest move for a young, copy-worth rock star and rock star's wife to make!

> **"Fuck you, everybody smokes during their pregnancy."**
> **Courtney Love**

"I didn't want to talk to VANITY FAIR," claimed Mrs Cobain. She felt that it was based on the "whole Madonna thing" and her marriage, that the magazine didn't normally cover rock musicians—and even so, she only sells 60,000 records. "What the fuck do they want with me?" She did the interview, she said, because "I was so sick of industry women talking and saying terrible things about me."

Tensions were mounting and yes, it would be pretty easy to be cynical about things. After all, there have been numerous occasions when the young newlyweds had put themselves so much in the firing line that you would have thought they had done it for the hell of it. But then again, look at things the other way. Take two young kids (because that's all they really are), shove them under the spotlight so fast that they haven't got a chance to breathe, and they're gonna make mistakes. It makes you wonder why someone couldn't just advise them them a little bit more. "The sickening politics that are involved with being a successful

> **"The sickening politics that are involved with being a successful commercial rock band are real aggravating. No one has any idea!"**
> **Kurt Cobain**

commercial rock band are real aggravating. No one has any idea!" said Cobain. Except for other successful, commercial rock bands, maybe! The key to it all is that you can't turn the clock back and you have to realign yourself to where you now are, because you have no choice.

Success changes everything
Nothing is the same for Nirvana any more. Not when you discover things like

Kurt caught in the
spotlight, on stage
and off.

MTV allegedly holding the band to ransom over their performance at the MTV Video Awards. Kurt and Courtney reckon that they were blackmailed over their appearance. If they didn't toe the line and do the decent thing, then neither Nirvana nor Hole videos would be rotated, nor any acts from the two bands' management roster, including Sonic Youth and the Beastie Boys.

How true this is no one can say for sure, but it must have scared the band to think that with the amount of power that they thought they had stumbled on for themselves, the only time the big boys really pay any attention to you is when you're a threat. And make no mistake,

> "People thought we'd self-destruct, but we haven't."
> **Chris Novoselic**

Nirvana are now a threat, faces and names known as well as Madonna (who, naturally, has had a run-in with Courtney!) and Michael Jackson.

"People thought we'd self-destruct, but we haven't," says Chris Novoselic, adding that he thought that too, because the band took off so suddenly. He felt that Nirvana were a lot tamer now, almost going through the motions. "What we need to do is put out a new record, play some new songs."

The one new song which saw the light of day on February 22, after the band had been down to Rio in Brazil to perform alongside L7 and the Red Hot Chili Peppers at the Hollywood Fest, was 'Oh, The Guilt', a none-too-inspiring workout written by Cobain and presented as part of the mooted split single with Jesus Lizard. The latter's contribution was titled 'Puss'.

While this one-off release might have been the most important event of the virgin year for many desperate for new Nirvana noise, to Chris Novoselic

it was just about the last thing on his mind. At the end of January he took a trip to Zagreb in Bosnia-Hercegovina, prompted by the news reports of the war that was raging there and deeply troubled by it because of his own family connections in the area.

Novoselic, who shortly after his visit changed his first name back to its original ethnic spelling of Krist, was appalled at the atrocities of war, especially the widespread

> "I don't want to play the rock 'n' roll pundit. I don't wanna be the guy who has something to say on every issue and play every benefit, 'cos that just isn't right. I'm not mentally capable of it. I'm just a bass player in a band."
>
> **Chris Novoselic**

Opposite: Sonic Youth, on Nirvana's management roster, were reportedly under threat of not having their videos rotated by MTV if Kurt and Courtney didn't toe the line at the MTV Video Awards.

rape of women, and was extremely vocal in his support for the Tresnjevka Women's Group, who help victims of this most heinous of crimes: "What we're basically doing", he stated, "is exploiting the media and the profile we have in the public eye, but in a positive way." Yet in typical Novoselic fashion, the lanky bassist was still wary of setting himself up as a spokesman for a generation: "I don't want to play the rock 'n' roll pundit. I don't wanna be the guy who has something to say on every issue and play every benefit, 'cos that just isn't right. I'm not mentally capable of it. I'm just a bass player in a band."

The new album

Shortly after Novoselic's return from Europe, the band finally headed out to the backwaters of Minnesota and the quirkiness of Steve Albini to commence work on the new album. After the speculation and the provocation, and nearly two years after the recording of NEVERMIND, Nirvana were finally back doing what they were meant to do—playing music with a fury, an anger, an intensity and a naïve joy. Music that connected way beyond their wildest dreams. Of course, the issue at stake now for the band was how they could redefine and reinvent themselves for IN UTERO.

Which brings us full circle to where we came into this tale of tales. With ructions with Albini. With rumours flying around that the band had been coerced into reworking certain mixes with Andy Wallace, the man who was responsible for giving NEVERMIND its commercial gloss. Ah, rumours, rumours—they're the stuff that the music industry thrives on.

Nirvana are easy grist to the star-making mill. It was the hype machine that made this band, but that same machine is working overtime to make sure that it gets its 10 cents' worth now. There's been talk of the band wilting under the pressure since just about the first day that NEVERMIND hit the ground running, and that talk has continued ever since. It's never going to stop, so the band might just as well get used to it.

Nirvana play music with fury, anger and a naïve joy.

The Nirvana enigma

Whatever you may think about Nirvana, you're going to have an opinion. Are they "Flower Sniffin', Kitty Pettin', Baby Kissin' Corporate Rock Whores", as the T-shirts that were sold after the band's success so ironically proclaimed? Or do Nirvana still have it in them to be radical? Don't ask me. If there's one thing you should get out of this book, it's that the band themselves don't even know where they stand. Confusion stands as high as anything on the Nirvana agenda, way above subversion, although granted they'd like a bit of that too. And why not? Do you expect a 26-year-old from Aberdeen to have it all sorted in his head?

What you can't take away from Nirvana are the solid gold facts. They have plugged a far more abrasive music than ever before into the mainstream consciousness, and they have certainly opened the potential in the minds of the meatheads that Cobain so abhors that "kick ass" rock 'n' roll bands can educate with an intelligent and liberal standpoint. You might not think that's

the most radical thing in the world, but then again, if you or I spent a bit of time in Aberdeen or any other two-bit American town just like it, then maybe we'd understand just a little better.

Wasters who came good

How much the reality of what they have lived through is going to affect Grohl, Novoselic and Cobain is impossible to assess. Cobain is under the most scrutiny and therefore has the harder job of handling it. Novoselic appears to have found other outlets for his energies which will hopefully funnel his attentions more positively.

And Grohl? Well, he's pretty cool about the whole thing. "I'm planning on having a life in a year or two," he says. To him, nothing that's happening makes sense. When he was young, he always thought of movie stars and rock stars as famous. But once it started happening to the band, it just destroyed that image—in Dave's words, "three scrawny little losers come out and sell a bunch of records." And you know, when you think about it, there's no better way of putting it, is there?

> **"Three scrawny little losers come out and sell a bunch of records."**
> **Dave Grohl**

Nirvana really are the wasters who came good.

Who can say why it was them and not one of a million others? Being in the right place at the right time? It sure has a lot to answer for. But maybe what happens now is that the middle ground of music has been stretched sufficiently to allow more uncompromising music to be heard by the mainstream. Not so there'll be a new Nirvana, but another, original form of exciting, contemporary, challenging music. And if that happens, then make sure you hitch up for the ride!

Kurt, Chris and Dave on stage: they challenged the rock establishment and came good.

Chronology

1986

Autumn

Kurt Cobain records a four-track demo with Melvins drummer Dale Crover, titled 'Fecal Matter'. Recruits Aaron Burkhart on drums and Chris Novoselic on bass. Nirvana begin gigging.

1988

Summer

Nirvana are spotted by Seattle independent label Sub Pop, who sign the band.

October

Nirvana release first single as part of Sub Pop's Singles Club series. 'Love Buzz'/'Big Cheese' is a limited edition of 1000.

December

With Chad Channing on drums Nirvana record début album, BLEACH, for $600 (£400). Guitarist Jason Everman is credited on the record, although he doesn't actually play on it.

1989

June

BLEACH is finally released on Sub Pop.

Summer

Jason Everman leaves the group.

Autumn

Nirvana play their first European dates in support of Sub Pop labelmates Tad.

1990

Spring   A proposed European tour is cancelled after disagreements with drummer Chad Channing, who leaves the band.

August   Nirvana tour the US with Dale Crover on drums.

September   'Sliver' single is released with Mudhoney's Dan Peters on drums.

December   With drumming problems permanently resolved with the hiring of erstwhile Scream member Dave Grohl, the band sign to Geffen Records.

1991

January   The band begin work on the major label début NEVERMIND, with Butch Vig producing. Andy Wallace will mix.

February   The final Sub Pop Nirvana single, 'Molly's Lips', is released.

August   The band performs at the prestigious Reading Festival in the UK.

September   NEVERMIND is released and sells out of its initial 50,000 pressing within days.

November   With Nirvana fever already in full effect, the band tours the UK. 'Smells Like Teen Spirit' crashes the UK singles charts. The album starts to explode.

1992

January   NEVERMIND knocks Michael Jackson's DANGEROUS off the Number 1 spot in the US BILLBOARD album chart.

February   Cobain marries pregnant girlfriend Courtney Love during the world tour, which has reached Japan and New Zealand.

April   Rumours of Cobain's supposed drug addiction persist. A ban on contact with the press is announced.

August   Killing Joke sue the band for allegedly filching parts of their songs. Frances Bean

Cobain is born on the 18th. Nirvana make a triumphant headlining return to the Reading Festival.

September   BLEACH is re-released. VANITY FAIR magazine prints pictures of a heavily pregnant and near-naked Courtney. Nirvana win two awards at the MTV awards show.

December   INCESTICIDE, a compilation of rarities, is released.

1993

January   It is confirmed that notorious producer Steve Albini (of Big Black fame) will produce the third Nirvana album, despite claims from the man that he wouldn't.

May   Having recorded the album, titled IN UTERO, Nirvana issue a statement denying that Geffen are interfering with the artistic content of the record after Albini has voiced concerns in a Chicago newspaper article. Cobain admits to remixing some tracks at the band's own insistence.

July   The band finally come out of recording hibernation to play a set at the New Music Seminar in New York, airing plenty of new material and introducing roadie "Big" John Duncan, erstwhile of the Exploited, as a supplementary guitarist on some live songs.

September   IN UTERO is finally released on the 13th. The world waits with bated breath.

Discography

US albums

Bleach
JUNE 1989
Sub Pop SP 34
Highest chart position: 89

Nevermind
OCTOBER 1991
Geffen DGC 24425
Highest chart position: 1

In Utero
SEPTEMBER 1993
Geffen DGC unconfirmed

singles

'Love Buzz'/'Big Cheese'
OCTOBER 1988
Did not chart

'Sliver'/'Dive'
SEPTEMBER 1990
Did not chart

'Molly's Lips'/'Fluid'
FEBRUARY 1991
Did not chart

'Here She Comes Now'
MARCH 1991
Did not chart

'Smells Like Teen Spirit'
OCTOBER 1991
Highest chart position: 6

'Come As You Are'
MARCH 1992
Highest chart position: 32

'Lithium'
JULY 1992
Highest chart position: 64

UK albums

Bleach
AUGUST 1989
Tupelo TUP LP6
Did not chart
RE-RELEASED MARCH 1992
Highest Chart Position: 33

Nevermind
SEPTEMBER 1991
Geffen DGC24425
Highest chart position: 33

In Utero
SEPTEMBER 1993
Geffen GED24536

singles

'Blew'/'Love Buzz'/ 'Been A Son'/'Stain'
DECEMBER 1989
Did not chart

'Sliver'/'Dive'/'About A Girl' (live)/'Spank Thru' (live)
JANUARY 1991
Did not chart

'Smells Like Teen Spirit'
NOVEMBER 1991
Highest chart position: 7

'Come As You Are'
MARCH 1992
Highest chart position: 9

'Lithium'
JULY 1992
Highest chart position: 11

'In Bloom'
DECEMBER 1992
Highest chart position: 28

Index

Index

Index

Picture acknowledgements

Photographs reproduced by kind permission of London Features International; Pictorial Press/Svenson; Redferns/Mick Hutson, Michael Linssen; Relay Photos; Retna/Matt Anker, /A. J. Barret, /Jay Blakesberg, /Jeff Davy, /A. Indge, /Neils Van Iperen, /Steve Pyke, /Chris Taylor, /Ian Tilton; Rex Features; Syndicated International Network.

Front cover picture: London Features International.